MW00608718

# Our Puget Sound
# Backyard Birds II

More of one couple's collection of candid bird photographs

Craig Johnson
Joy Johnson

Special Edition
1250 copies on first press run

**ORANGE SPOT PUBLISHING**

# PREFACE

Natives of western Washington, Craig and Joy grew up sailing, camping and hiking around the beautiful Puget Sound area. This connection to nature persisted for them as adults and has become an integral part of their relationship, continually leading them to explore the outdoors.

While not advocates of caging birds, many years ago they acquired a cockatiel as a nestling. Caring for this bird for more than a decade, regularly observing her behaviors and unique characteristics, increased their knowledge and appreciation of birds in general. Feeding wild birds in the backyard spurred their curiosity to find out more about each bird that came by, which led them to study bird biology through the Cornell Lab of Ornithology and to go out birding multiple times each week.

As a watercolor artist with a marine art business, Craig was accustomed to photographing vessels as research material from which to paint. It was natural for him to begin photographing birds as they stopped by their home feeders and while out in the field. Using a 400mm, f/4-f/5.6 lens, all photos were taken without a tripod or monopod. These images aided Craig with his avian paintings, many becoming artistic works on their own. With enough photos compiled to create a book, Joy applied her research and writing skills to the text.

After quickly selling out their first book, *Our Puget Sound Backyard Birds*, Craig and Joy wanted to create another edition to continue sharing the pleasure they have experienced in their birding adventures. *Our Puget Sound Backyard Birds II* contains the addition of several bird species, some different locations, and new photos of the wide assortment of local birds found in their first book. Both books were printed in the northwest with very low press-runs. As supporters of wildlife preservation organizations, they will commit proceeds from the sales of this book to these efforts.

Watercolor of a male Northern Flicker by Craig Johnson

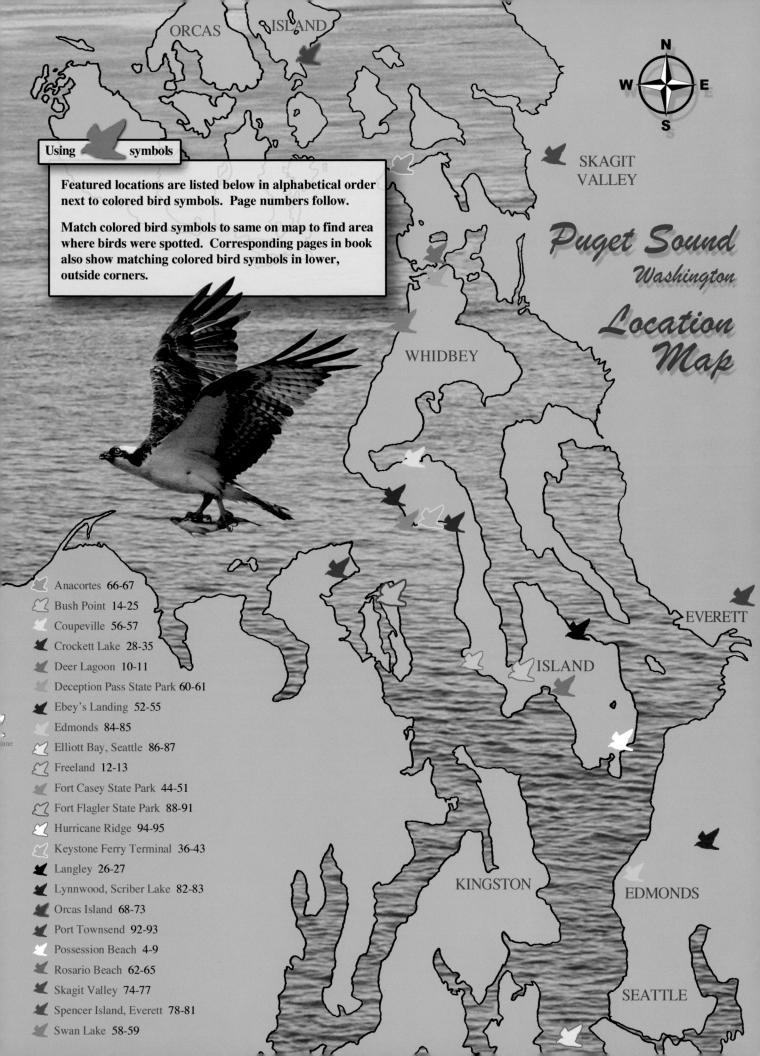

ORCAS ISLAND

N
W E
S

SKAGIT VALLEY

*Puget Sound*
*Washington*

*Location Map*

WHIDBEY

**Using** symbols

Featured locations are listed below in alphabetical order next to colored bird symbols. Page numbers follow.

Match colored bird symbols to same on map to find area where birds were spotted. Corresponding pages in book also show matching colored bird symbols in lower, outside corners.

EVERETT

ISLAND

KINGSTON

EDMONDS

SEATTLE

Western Tanager, male

Western Tanager, female

Observing wild birds is a continual progression. Once we become familiar with one species, there is another to get to know. When we have identified all of the birds in our yard, the next place to look is the local park. Then there are other parks in the vicinity, nature reserves throughout the state, and so on. It is a lifelong adventure.

**Possession Beach**, on southern Whidbey Island, is one park where we like to look for birds. With shoreline, marsh, and wooded areas, there are a variety of species found here. Some are residents all year and others just visit during their annual migration.

Western Tanager, juvenile

Ruby-crowned Kinglet

Willow Flycatcher

Olive-sided Flycatcher with Dragonfly

Perched like a tree-topper, the Olive-sided Flycatcher surveys the area. True to form, it captures a large dragonfly.

Barn Swallow, juvenile

Summer is the time to look for swallows in the park as they come here to breed. We spotted the Ruby-crowned Kinglet and Golden-crowned Sparrow in the fall.

Violet-green Swallow

Golden-crowned Sparrow

Ruby-crowned Kinglet

Cedar Waxwing

Horned Grebe

Horned Grebe, breeding

From the beach marine birds are sometimes visible, like the Horned Grebes above; one is exhibiting non-breeding and the other breeding plumage.

A Double-crested Cormorant can often be found perched on a piling at the end of the dock.

**Double-crested Cormorant**

Rhinoceros Auklet with several fish

Rhinoceros Auklet

Some Rhinoceros Auklets are year-round inhabitants of Puget Sound. Clearly adept at catching fish, the adult will clutch about six of them between its upper mandible and its very specialized, stiff tongue until nightfall when it will venture ashore to feed its young chick.

Rhinoceros Auklet, breeding

Western Grebe

Red-necked Grebe, breeding

Red-necked Grebe

Lesser Yellowlegs

Greater Yellowlegs

Expansive mudflats exposed during low tide attract shorebirds like these Greater and Lesser Yellowlegs at **Deer Lagoon**. They forage in the shallow water for aquatic worms, small fish and crustaceans with their long, probing beaks.

It was a treat to watch this Green Heron so clearly fixated on hunting as its young squawked from a hidden location in the nearby cattails, demanding to be fed. By remaining still and silent, we were able to avoid startling this vigilant bird.

Rufous Hummingbird, female collecting nesting material

Yellow-rumped Warbler, male

At the Earth Sanctuary, a privately owned nature reserve near **Freeland**, numerous birds take advantage of its protected atmosphere. Ducklings of many varieties can be observed paddling behind their parents during late spring and into summer.

Wood Duck, male

Wood Duck, female with ducklings

Brown-headed Cowbird, juvenile

Brown-headed Cowbird, male

The environment here is thoughtfully sculpted around the wildlife, with immense consideration given to the needs of nesting birds. Tranquility is almost tangible as you sit quietly and let your senses absorb nature.

Red-breasted Sapsucker

Red-breasted Sapsucker, juvenile

Red-breasted Sapsucker

As the weather gets warmer, our yard at **Bush Point** becomes as colorful as an artist's palette, attracting migrating hummingbirds and more.

American Goldfinch, male

Anna's Hummingbird, female

Rufous Hummingbird, male

Rufous Hummingbird, male

Rufous Hummingbird, female

The enchanting sounds of birds bursting into song, attempting to attract their mates, can be heard throughout the yard in the springtime.

Bewick's Wren

Later in the summer, we watch for fledglings to show themselves. Often they can be spotted trailing their parents and crying to be fed.

Bewick's Wren, juvenile

Bushtit, female

Purple Finch, female

Purple Finch, male

A variety of woodpeckers regularly visits our yard, hunting for insects on the trees as well as stopping at the suet feeder for an easy snack.

Pileated Woodpecker, male

Hairy Woodpecker, male

Hairy Woodpecker, male & Northern Flicker, female

Most of the birds that frequent our yard like to sample the suet once in a while. It is especially appealing to them in winter when the weather is cold and food is scarce.

Red-breasted Nuthatch, male

Northern Flicker, female feeding a juvenile

Adult birds continue to feed their fledglings until they learn to forage for themselves, as this flicker pair demonstrates. Young birds that are raised utilizing birdfeeders will also learn to forage for natural foods found in the wild.

Red Crossbill, male

Northern Flicker, male

Having feeders in the yard can bring some less common birds in for a closer view, like these colorful Red Crossbills. Their unique bill configuration is ideally suited for extracting seeds from pine and fir cones, but they also like to eat sunflower seeds.

Red Crossbill, female

Band-tailed Pigeon

Steller's Jay

Providing a clean birdbath with fresh water is another way to attract birds to your yard, as a consistent water source is important.

What a pleasure it is to watch birds splash in the refreshing water as they drink and bathe!

Varied Thrush, male

Spotted Towhee, male

Evening Grosbeak, male

Backyard landscaping that is designed in layers will allow birds the natural areas they need for cover when a predator appears. With a variety of indigenous trees, shrubs, and ground plants, birds can find food as well as necessary protection.

Black-headed Grosbeak, female

Black-headed Grosbeak, male

Osprey

Hybrid Glaucous-winged / Western Gull

Mourning Dove, female & male

Great Blue Heron

Strolling along the beach near our home, we find the soothing, steady sounds of water lapping on the shore to be a refreshing respite from work. Looking for birds that might pop up from under the water or fly overhead has become second nature to us as we walk.

Red-breasted Mergansers, molting

Golden-crowned Sparrow

Northern Rough-winged Swallow

Western Sandpipers

**Langley** is a small, quaint town on the southern portion of Whidbey Island. You never know what you might find on the beach at Seawall Park; these Western Sandpipers were foraging right at the base of the stairs.

Mew Gulls

Barred Owl

**Crockett Lake** on Central Whidbey is one of our favorite places to look for birds. At first glance the area may seem barren, but with a keen eye (and the help of binoculars), one can see that it is teaming with wildlife. From large, formidable raptors to small sparrows, birds abound here in the grasses, at the water's edge, and on the water. Species that can be seen here change with the seasons, so there is always the potential of something new

Short-eared Owl

Savannah Sparrow

Western Meadowlark

Northern Harrier, female

Snowy Owl

Northern Harrier, male & Red-winged Blackbird, male

Short-eared Owl

Northern Pintail, male & female

Brewer's Blackbird, male

Belted Kingfisher, female

A mix of birds can be found in various habitat areas around the lake. Standing out from the rest are birds perched on pilings and fence posts, like the owl, hawk and kingfisher.

Red-tailed Hawk, juvenile

Long-billed Curlew

Great Blue Heron, adult & juvenile

Red-winged Blackbird, male

Northern Shrike

Short-eared Owl

The open setting here provides space for
a multitude of creatures to live and feed.
Insects and seeds nourish many smaller
birds and mammals, who may then become
a meal for larger birds of prey.

Brewer's Blackbird, female

Red-tailed Hawk

Common Raven

Northern Harrier, female with wing tag

Northern Harrier, male

Dunlin

Northern Harriers can be seen swooping low over the marsh all year long. Spring and fall migrations bring a stream of shorebirds traveling through. Mid-summer is the time to look for Caspian Terns gathered here after breeding elsewhere.

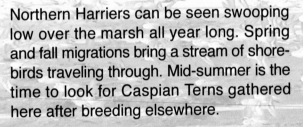
Least Sandpiper

Caspian Terns

Long-billed Dowitchers

Long-billed Dowitcher

Peregrine Falcon

The Merlin, a solitary hunter, can fly with impressive agility. Small shorebirds must be on guard for this stealthy predator. When startled, shorebirds will fly evasively as a flock, turning with amazing precision in a collective effort to confuse and distract their assailant.

Merlin, female

Greater Yellowlegs

Pigeon Guillemot, adult & yearling

Pigeon Guillemot, juvenile with crustacean

Pigeon Guillemots can be seen regularly in the summertime, sunning themselves on the rocks and on the old pier, at **Keystone State Park** near the ferry landing. Very gregarious birds, they nest in colonies and are quite spirited, with bright red mouths and feet.

Pigeon Guillemot

Pigeon Guillemot, non-breeding

Pigeon Guillemot, "all dark" (uncommon)

Pigeon Guillemot

Common Murre, molting

Red-necked Phalarope, non-breeding

Marbled Murrelet

Just offshore in Keystone Harbor and to the south along the coast, many marine birds can be distinguished with binoculars or a scope.

Barrow's Goldeneye & Red-necked Grebe

Red-breasted Merganser, female

Surf Scoter, male & female

Harlequin Ducks

On the edge of the shore, we sometimes see a Bald Eagle perched on the driftwood, perhaps awaiting a tidal change for optimal fishing conditions.

Least Sandpipers and Black Oystercatchers find the rocky shore an appealing place to find a meal, while the Great Blue Heron feeds on fish in the nearby water.

Least Sandpiper, juvenile

Great Blue Heron

Black Oystercatcher

It was enjoyable to watch a group of Western Sandpipers taking a break to rest and preen in the balmy summer sunshine.

Bonaparte's Gull

California Gull

Hybrid Glaucous-winged / Western Gulls

Great Blue Heron chick

Great Blue Heron with chick

Glaucous-winged Gull chicks

Great Blue Heron on nest

Some birds, like this heron and gull, will make nests right on top of the huge pilings at the ferry landing. Surprisingly, they are quite tolerant of the noise and traffic that the ferry brings at regular intervals.

Glaucous-winged Gull on nest

In the wooded area of **Fort Casey State Park**, behind Admiralty Head Lighthouse, we have noted evidence of woodpeckers chipping away at snags. Typically we hear the tapping and calling before we actually spot one of the several species that are active here.

Downy Woodpecker, male

Pileated Woodpecker, male

Northern Flicker, male

Brown Creeper

Orange-crowned Warbler

On the ground and in the underbrush, we might see a Spotted Towhee foraging among the leaves while a Brown Creeper works its way up the tree trunk, both searching for unwary arthropods.

Spotted Towhee, male

The *chick-a-dee-dee-dee* of the chickadee's song sounds cheerful and distinctive. A curious and bold bird, it is often visible working the branches of a tree even when other birds retreat.

Black-capped Chickadee

Chestnut-backed Chickadee

Small birds, like this Dark-eyed Junco, must always be watchful for predators such as the Sharp-shinned Hawk.

Sharp-shinned Hawk, adult

It was fascinating to monitor the progress of a family of Great Horned Owls in the park throughout the summer. The young owlets were initially quite vocal. Never far from their parent, we observed them resting and preening together.

Great Horned Owl, juvenile

Great Horned Owl, adult & juvenile preening

Yellow-rumped Warbler, adult male

Yellow-rumped Warblers flit around, up and down trees, gleaning insects. Occasionally one will dart out of the branches in hot pursuit of a flying bug.

Yellow-rumped Warbler, juvenile male

To our delight, some birds will actually come closer to check us out as we stand quietly observing them.

Golden-crowned Kinglet, male

Common Raven

Lincoln's Sparrow

Merlin, female

Farm fields around the **Ebey's Landing** area sometimes host birds looking for a meal in the newly worked earth.

American Goldfinch, male & female

Bald Eagle, juvenile

Ebey's Landing State Park has magnificent vistas of Puget Sound, Olympic and Cascade Mountains from the bluff trail.

Black Turnstones

Caspian Tern

Along the shore, we were surprised to see a Whimbrel on the beach.

Marine birds sometimes pop up close to shore when busy searching for a meal.

Horned Grebe, spring

Whimbrel

Whimbrel

Heading toward **Coupeville** on Parker Road, we have regularly viewed this elegant female American Kestrel and occasionally a male, possibly her mate, perched on the fence posts or telephone poles.

American Kestrel, male

American Kestrel, female

In front of the Coupeville Museum, we recorded a rare visit by this Palm Warbler.

Palm Warbler

Common Loon

Common Loon with crab

From the historic pier and waterfront, marine and shorebirds are visible, including an occasional Ruddy Turnstone.

Ruddy Turnstone

Marsh Wren

Bucolic **Swan Lake** in Oak Harbor has a variety of habitats, inviting to a wide array of birds.

Killdeer

Common Goldeneye, female

Lesser Yellowlegs

The freshwater/saltwater mix here, which leaves muddy areas exposed at low tide, is appealing to numerous shorebirds during their migration.

Short-billed Dowitcher, juvenile

House Finch, male

Pileated Woodpecker, juvenile

Osprey

**Deception Pass State Park**, at the northern end of Whidbey Island, boasts saltwater beaches, old growth forest, and a freshwater lake, which attract a broad assortment of birdlife.

Common Loon, non-breeding

Olive-sided Flycatcher with Bumblebee

Wilson's Warbler, male

Willow Flycatcher

**Rosario Beach State Park** on the Fidalgo Island side of the Deception Pass Bridge has breathtaking views, like this one of Rosario Strait, from its trails and beaches. We saw a pair of Black Oystercatchers on various large rocks along the shore all through the summer.

Black Oystercatcher

The Downy Woodpecker has black and white head stripes similar to those of the White-crowned Sparrow.

This curious sparrow hopped out to the end of a branch as if to greet us when we walked past on a trail.

Downy Woodpecker, female

This attractive American Robin shows the lighter colored plumage typical of female robins compared to the darker gray-black and brighter reddish colors of the male pictured on the next page. The juvenile has a dark spotted breast and light speckled back.

American Robin, juvenile

American Robin, female

American Robin, juvenile

American Robin, male

Turkey Vulture

Purple Martin houses

**Anacortes**, *Gateway to the San Juan Islands*, has some great birding locations. Near the ferry terminal, the beach hosts a variety of birds as well as a man-made nesting area for Purple Martins on the old pilings.

Rock Pigeon

Tree Swallow

Belted Kingfisher, female

Where there was once bustling industry in this historic town, birds have turned what remains into workable accommodations. Adaptation is often key to survival in the bird world.

Glaucous-winged Gull

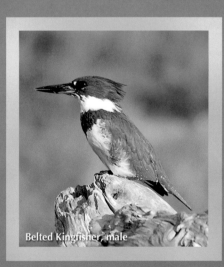

Belted Kingfisher, male

Great Blue Heron

American Goldfinch, juvenile

On **Orcas Island**, the wooded areas of Moran State Park are a haven for many species of passerines (perching birds).

Winter Wren

White-crowned Sparrow; juvenile & adult

American Goldfinch, male

Hermit Thrush

Golden-crowned Kinglet, male

Lush, cool greenery surrounds you as you walk into the woods, while the birds' cheerful music graces your ears.

At our family's cabin near Doe Bay, we have been fortunate to have opportunities to get up close to birds. The natural grounds around the unobtrusive cabin, built in 1962, invite scores of wild creatures.

Song Sparrow

California Quail feed on the ground, usually in a group, with an adult male lookout keeping watch for predators. The male is distinguishable from the female by his larger crest.

California Quail, male

California Quail, female

Pine Siskin will come to backyard feeders, particularly enjoying niger and sunflower seeds.

A House Wren makes a claim on a birdhouse by standing on the roof and periodically singing, as well as fending off any competing birds.

House Wren

Pine Siskin

Spotted Towhee, adult male

The juvenile Spotted Towhee has dull, brownish plumage, helping it to blend with its nesting area. An adult male towhee has well defined black, rufous and white feather coloring with distinctive red eyes.

Spotted Towhee, juvenile

Osprey

Bald Eagle

The **Skagit Valley** is an expansive area offering many great birding opportunities.

Great Blue Heron

Northern Harrier, female

Ring-necked Pheasant, male

Greater White-fronted Goose

Snow Goose

Trumpeter Swans, juveniles & adults

In the winter this area is attractive to many migrating species including a wide variety of waterfowl.

Pied-billed Grebe

Northern Shoveler, male

75

Northern Shrike

Gyrfalcon

Driving along the farm roads in the Skagit Valley, it is common to spy raptors perched upon the telephone poles or wires. Surveying the scene from an elevated viewpoint can be advantageous when looking for prey.

Rough-legged Hawk

Peregrine Falcon

Cooper's Hawk, juvenile

Red-tailed Hawk, juvenile

Mallard, female & ducklings

**Spencer Island** in north Everett is a bit hard to find, but well worth the effort. The reserve area, where hunting is not allowed, offers ample walking trails and a variety of easily visible habitat areas. We observed many "first time" species here, including the Eastern Kingbird.

Willow Flycatcher

Eastern Kingbird

Spotted Sandpiper, juvenile

Cinnamon Teal, male

Great Blue Heron

American Bittern

An American Bittern surprised us by suddenly flying up from the marsh nearby as we walked along the dike. It landed out some distance away and began to sway like the reeds and grass around it.

American Bittern

Canada Geese, adults & goslings

Yellow Warbler, male

Bullock's Oriole, male

Bullock's Oriole, female

Many colorful migratory birds either breed in this area or just pass through. The Bullock's Oriole was another bird we saw here for the first time.

This stunning juvenile Red-tailed Hawk was perched on a snag and then flew right over the trail where we were walking, showing off its broad underwings.

Red-tailed Hawk, juvenile

Bufflehead, male

Hooded Merganser, male

American Wigeon, male & female

Many different types of ducks stop off at Scriber Lake Park in **Lynnwood** during their spring and fall migrations.

Mallard, male

American Coot

Small perching birds, like the Winter Wren,
may pop up out of the underbrush.

We were thrilled to observe Green Heron
successfully nesting here.

Green-winged Teal, male

Green Heron, juvenile

Winter Wren

The exuberant song of a Marsh Wren makes a pleasant welcome to the **Edmonds** Marsh. More elusive is the Virginia Rail, foraging on the ground among shadowy reeds.

Marsh Wren

Virginia Rail

Belted Kingfisher, male

Brant

Edmonds waterfront has regulars like the Belted Kingfisher and American Crow. It may also have visiting species, like these Brant riding the waves at Brackett's Landing Park.

Purple Martin, female

Purple Martin, male

Double-crested Cormorant

Canada Goose

Glaucous Gull

Jack Block Park in West Seattle has some impressive views of **Elliott Bay** and downtown Seattle. A number of birds have adapted to living in this urban, industrial environment, including a group of Purple Martins making use of man-made nesting cavities.

Great Blue Heron

Belted Kingfisher, male

**Fort Flagler State Park**
on Marrowstone Island provides
opportunities for passerines to
find shelter and forage in the
trees and shrubs.

Cedar Waxwing, juvenile

Yellow-rumped Warbler, female

Townsend's Warbler

Wilson's Warbler, male

We spotted our first Wilson's Warbler here and then proceeded to watch a group of them working the bushes, flying from one area to another and back again for quite some time.

Wilson's Warbler, female

The tiny Orange-crowned Warblers pictured were completely engrossed in watching insects crawling on nearby leaves.

Orange-crowned Warbler, with ant

Orange-crowned Warbler

Ruby-crowned Kinglet

House Sparrow, male

Bushtit, male

Common Yellowthroat, male

These diminutive birds are insectivorous and zip about in pursuit of prey, with the exception of the House Sparrow, which is primarily a seed eater.

**Port Townsend** has an active waterfront bird population. These Killdeer were nesting in an area protected by fencing.

Killdeer

This juvenile Black-bellied Plover blends perfectly into its rocky beach environment. The adult displays the descriptive black breeding plumage on its belly.

Black-bellied Plover

Black-bellied Plover, juvenile

Though not part of Puget Sound, **Hurricane Ridge** in the nearby Olympic Mountains is a great place to look for birds in the summertime. American Pipits are common around the lodge at the top of the ridge.

American Pipit

On the way down the mountain, we spotted this Sooty Grouse (formerly called Blue Grouse), who is clearly adapted for camouflage in this environment.

Sooty Grouse, female

Bird watching can help us reconnect with the many wonders of our natural world as our society is increasingly enclosed indoors. Whether we record what we see with photos, a journal, or just hold onto the memories, the experiences can be invaluable.

**Happy birding!**

Gray Jay

## Acknowledgements

Special thanks to Frances Wood, author of *Brushed by Feathers*: *A Year of Birdwatching in the West*, writer of an award-winning newspaper column about birdwatching, and President of the Whidbey Audubon Society. Her assistance and contributions were greatly appreciated.

Thanks also to Dennis Paulson, author of *Shorebirds of the Pacific Northwest*, for sharing his expertise, which was very helpful.

Our gratitude is also extended to the wonderful people who proofread the book in its various stages before publication.

## References

The Birds Of North America Online, Cornell Lab of Ornithology and the American Ornithologists Union. 2004-2005
www.bna.birds.cornell.edu

BirdWeb, Seattle Audubon Society, 2005. www.birdweb.org

Peterson, Roger Tory & Virginia Marie Peterson, *A Field Guide to Western Birds, 3rd ed.*, Boston/NewYork: Houghton Mifflin Company, 1990.

Podulka, Sandy, Ronald W. Rohrbaugh, Jr., and Rick Bonney, Eds., *Handbook of Bird Biology, 2nd Ed.* Ithaca: Princeton University Press, 2004.

Sibley, David Allen, *The Sibley Field Guide to Birds of Western North America*, New York: Alfred A. Knopf, 2003.

Photographs, graphics & layout by Craig Johnson. Written by Joy Johnson. All photographs were taken with 400 mm, f/4 & f/5.6 lenses. Photographs have not been altered other than in page layout.

Bird identification was typically based on a series of photos taken of different angles of the same bird, not just the one photo shown in this book.

For more information on bird watching and bird feeding, contact your local Audubon Society and Wild Bird Store.

Great Horned Owl